salmonpoetry

Publishing Irish & International
Poetry Since 1981

the arts council
chomhairle
ealaíon

funding
literature

artscouncil.ie

How the Weather Was
Jean Kavanagh

Published in 2019 by
Salmon Poetry
Cliffs of Moher, County Clare, Ireland
Website: www.salmonpoetry.com
Email: info@salmonpoetry.com

ISBN 978-1-912561-55-1

Cover & Title Page Photograph: Jean Kavanagh

Cover Design & Typesetting: *Siobhán Hutson*

Printed in Ireland by Sprint Print

*Salmon Poetry gratefully acknowledges the support of
The Arts Council / An Chomhairle Ealaíon*

For
Leonard

Acknowledgments

I want to thank my family for their continued support and insight, and particularly to my brother Barry for his help with this manuscript.

To my teachers, classmates and friends in Tromsø, ollu giitu for two fantastic years up North, and to the Norwegian government for funding my Master's degree.

To everyone in Oslo, mostly for just being yourselves, but especially for the help with finishing this book: Mikkel for the chillout time on Nesodden; Itta and Aslak for the respite in Fredrikstad; and of course to Jarl and Tom Kenneth for the roof over my head in Kalbakken, and all the poetry on the balcony.

As always, to Jessie and Siobhán of Salmon Poetry, for two fantastic summer writing residencies above the bookshop in Ennistymon in Clare, and for everything else you do for me and all the other Salmon poets.

I would also like to acknowledge the family and friends of Julie Ryan, her life made us all part of the same story. 'Funeral Rain' is my version of this story. I hope I have your blessing.

All good books are alike in that they are truer than if they had really happened and after you are finished reading one you will feel that all that happened to you and afterwards it all belongs to you: the good and the bad, the ecstasy, the remorse and sorrow, the people and the places and how the weather was...

ERNEST HEMINGWAY

Contents

Semesters in Snow

Incarnate

Gandhi meditates on the lawn
of the Peace Studies building
on campus, in Tromsø.
He enjoys his part
in university life;
students come to visit
his quiet fame,
sit on the grass,
and keep him abreast
of current affairs.

One late night in November,
he saw lights in the window,
the flash of a map
on a big screen,
and heard the sounds
of student protest.

She came running outside
when Florida turned red,
as if the building
had caught fire,
and implored him,
Please, Gandhi, please,
tell me he won't win.

He looked over his glasses,
and into her eyes,
said, not unkindly,

You don't understand
History.

And now, the winter snows
fall onto words
spoken by a statue's ghost
and cover Ghandi's metal
head and shoulders like a cloak

and muffle ears
from soundings of the past
becoming future cries,
old fears spin to new lies until
all of this turns over
into the certain spring
of changing terms.
Then she comes to see
the thawed outcome
of his prophecy.

Sállir

I.

The night bus traverses
a bridge between islands,
brings me back from a day
where I was being myself
and almost pulled it off.
No one is looking
here for me yet,
no place to miss me
all the time,
another unpacking
of what is mine.

II.

A mountain at my back,
yesterday
there were reindeer
down by my feet
at the shore.
Last night
the Northern Lights
danced, and I saw
their purple petticoats
beneath the hem of green,
scarves of light
that rippled in and out
among themselves
in an Arctic sky,
a music with no sound.

III.

I have formed a friendship
with the view.
It changes every day;
mountains can be seen,
then unseen,
clarity and cloud,
the coloured sea
from pale haze
to charcoal frown,
as seasons turn the land
from white, to brown, to green.

IV.

Behind the kitchen window,
fridge poetry and a red tablecloth,
cooking in domestic waltz,
I know the distance
to knives in drawers,
and timings on the hob;
and taking copper pots
out of their shine
those last few times,
I knew
that home is this,
to miss
moving in this space.

Storelva

Here inside
my student room of snow,
there are no pictures
for the walls, no portals
to my other lives.
I live inside the circle
they call the Arctic
of the Earth,
and North is everywhere;
so I become my own
solitary point,
a pole, a star,
bring myself home
over ice
to a purpose
of fire,
where great things
have a hiding place
within an attic room.
I will find them,
I will be safe and warm.

Daylight Saving Time

A Norwegian dawn
is a foolish thing,
a pale light
that comes too early,
stays too long,
or doesn't come at all;
moving through
our constant evenings,
surprised to find
the sun in different places,
as if the clock
has lied to us,
telling the same time.

Only twice a year,
changing back
or forward
the hands on a face,
do we notice
how we move;
day and night
in equal measure,
but unevenly dispersed,
in shadow-circles
on the earth.

The Colour of Love

Sometimes, when I talk of love,
I see a little blue light
through the trees
in the distance,
that was you.
If I go closer,
and look in the window,
there is a fire burning,
that makes everything orange,
that was us,
in the glow;
I wonder,
living, then,
did I ever see
my future self
pressed up
against the glass,
and know.

Frost

I needed a win, today,
but this year
has not been kind;
at the bar, I am
another dialect,
I am the stranger
on the last bus home,
I am
my frozen fingers
in the snow.

Yes, people love me,
but their timing
isn't always right;
left to my own
impaired device,
in the small hours
of one night.

The Yellow House

Those who remember the darkness
can find themselves being a guest,
could wake up the host to ask,
Where is a candle?
but think it more
of an adventure to guess.

The darkness reminds them
they once hid under covers
from spirits, looming over
the ends of their beds;
invoked Catholic Jesus
and Leonard Cohen,
in song-prayers,
like a curtain's fall
between the Otherworld
and the Dead.

They remember then the hypnotic eye
deep in the ruby of wine,
a light in the corners
of kind company,
in distance of hours
from day time.

Now, they don't need
to leave the light on,
having learnt to come home
to a table,
to a chair,
to a bed;
a haven's embrace
that leans on the night,
and dawn enters in
on a yellow thread.

Street Level

To smoke, I stand outside,
a Friday night is five steps down
from the front door.
Almost over now, the city centre's
slow exodus begins, voices passing by
in rise and ebb of sound.

A couple, hand in hand
walk by, that seem to know
each other's step, the girl
looks up at me
and smiles, her eyes say,

Hi! I'm happy,
hope you're happy too,
I can't see
another possibility
for you, because
I'm going home with my man,
a perfect end to our night,
so all must be right
with the world,
for you, as well as me.

I don't know what
in that split second
my eyes answer,
either way,
what is my honesty?
Looking into
the soul of a girl
I used to be.

Paper Fish

We who are scattered
are loose pages
fallen from books,
libraries of letters
stashed in the attics,
old diaries in places
we can't bear to look.

We became sirens
to our own ship's manifest,
feel the pull, like an ache
for the sound of the sea,
anchored in hope
in a sound between shores,
we know how to swim
for the rocks
in an oncoming storm.

Wish Upon a Star

I want more time, more youth
for all ambition's needs,
can't bear the thought
that it might be
too late for fortune, smiling on
the bravado of the young,
with me beside them
oh so mature
weighing every word
and so unsure,
standing, hands on hips
above myself saying,
You can do this!

And I do.

Looking up I see the stars,
I know their reach,
then looking down I see
within the glitter of the ice,
the stars
are also at my feet.

Married to my Thesis

I was in love
with the idea of you,
and oh, the plans we made.
It was all going to be
so perfect;
but slowly my life
became your ultimatum.
Possessive of my time,
you didn't let me see
my family or friends
unless they were somehow
connected to you.
I give you all my days,
you make me feel guilty
if I take a night off,
coming in late, you are there
in the dark, in your
passive-aggressive armchair,
saying,
We'll talk about this in the morning.

But the end is in sight;
I will make beautiful
my plight, submit my case,
get a hearing within
a deadline's power,
and win back custody
and validation
of every hour.

Hufsa (The Groke)

Down from the mountain
she comes, to find
the company of other souls,
hope in front of her,
behind, her past
a trail of ice, unspoken
in her wake.
A clumsy smile
too many teeth
make sinister,
misunderstood,
her fragile bulk
a hill between the trees,
watching other bright
things play
with the thing she lost
she knew she once had,
beautiful, but reaching for it, finds
the fear in others' eyes,
wanting for herself the jewel
of a lady's due.

And oh, the sea
she'd row across,
to the island home
of her creator,
make her plea,
for sleight of hand
of pen to paper:

Write another story,
the tale of Lonely Mountains,
with wonder, warmth,
and sympathy,
where the circle of the glow
I crave
returns to me.

The Eighth of March

Born on a windy day, I share
the date with my namesake,
and all women, everywhere.
This year, it was cake for lunch
in the reading rooms, a beer
in the college bar,
I'd been good so long
I needed to rebel, so instead
of the Women's Day march in town,
I grabbed my Padawan, and
we made tracks
for the brownest bar I knew
for pints
in the afternoon;
after all,
it was my birthday too.

We talked about friendship
and looming futures,
got drunk enough
to get matching tattoos,
that say
Only the Wise Make Mistakes
in Elvish,
but postponed the moment
until we could decide
between Quenya and Sindarin.

We tangoed through the door
of a missed dinner
with our frozen pizza,
rejoined our abandoned friends,
and were delightfully obnoxious
with tales of adventures,
two souls far from home,
and here, in this city,
magnificent
to the end.

Soft Day Thank God

The only thing
up here in spring
that melts
the winter stockpile
of the snow
is wind and rain.
I'm back in Irish weather.
Air feels like home,
damp
and mild
and fierce
with recognition;
something that
I own again.

Not Quite

Maybe it's not you
who will keep me up
beneath the slanted roof
with music, and talking
the books from the shelf,
in ways that fascinate
some bright winter longing
that had gathered the dust
of a life so far.

The hour came and went,
but never quite arrived,
like dawn on an island
where the sun doesn't
set in June;
and night must be carried
within, to remember
the joy of first light.

The Ballad of Tromsø

If I found the music,
I would come home tonight
and write your song;
an Arctic island city
surrounded by the mountains
that, at first,
I could not take in
with just my eyes,
new shapes of rhyme,
and yet my own tune
still keeps time.

This may not be
an ending-place, for me,
too busy in my head
for feet to feel beneath
the frozen earth,
but friends I've made
were more than just enough.

I go to the hills
to ask for answers
that live within my choices,
and the mountains promised
they would hold me
until I need to go;
but said
I might not find
the thing I really love,
not here,
not in the snow.

Mozart's Mass in C Minor

The violins of the *Kyrie*
are a butterfly
loose, in the ceremony
of a church,
a slow flutter of wings
in a sacred space;
beauty, sure of what it is,
that 'cellos know and answer
around the other instruments,
a choir in four-part
harmonies of human voice,
calling to their human god
to hear.
It dances through their music,
and around,
doesn't need to ask
and joins in anyway,
alighting on the altar
to hear the soprano sing.
She is the angel
that holds pure sound,
a power where all praise,
all prayers, come together.

The butterfly
comments and questions
everything, argues
with the tenors and the altos
and the bass,
there are deep discussions,
points argued through,
voice and violin
that come quietly down
to a conclusion;
joy is the answer,
all is harmony.

In this adventure
in our own church
at the altar of each desk,
we create a curiosity
that comes only
with passion,
and struggle to be
Mozart's butterflies;
dancing with our words
like the hidden
mathematics of music,
we work hard
to make it effortless,
add the rhythm
of our own wings,
and make space
to sing soprano.

Class Dismissed

We fly away in silver birds
as others circle, land,
and come to take our place.
I return to Oslo,
and my Sámi friend remarks,
You're going back to Norway!

I am not sorry,
not sad to go.
How can I be?
These people
these mountains
all the knowledge gained
are worn like the sun
on a silver brooch;
I cannot miss them
if I take them with me.

Sunny Spells

Sea Glass

A sea bird dives
into the mirror
of the fjord,
seeks its prize,
as if there is no border
between water
and the air.

And on Langøyene,
we look for our
own treasures,
unearth forgotten jewels –
the right words
caressed into the quiet,
cloud-shadows
caught up in sunset,
and that minute, after,
where the sea
is brighter than the sky.

I was woken,
like to the sound of rain
falling on the camp;
found inside a moment,
an end unto itself, intense,
but not without reward.

There are scattered
keepsakes
on the shore –
complete again,
in smaller pieces;
opaque, worn smooth,
no longer fragile,
yet still transparent
at their heart.

Parallel Universe

She encountered an architect
while backpacking around Europe
with her best friend from school
in their twenties;
he'd read all the same books,
and was up for adventure.
He proposed in New York
with a Tiffany's ring,
and she loves him,
this I know.

He inherited
a falling-down house
from a great-aunt
on Avoca Avenue.
They moved into it,
room by room;
and over the years
they lovingly discovered
floorboards under mouldy carpets,
they replastered walls,
and replaced the shutters
on Victorian windows.

She gave her kids Irish names,
and drives them to a gaelscoil
every morning
in an old VW Beetle convertible
she bought for a song
in the Nineties
that always breaks down,
and when people say
Would you ever give up that oul' car?
she laughs,
her father's daughter.

She buys good wine
and has dinner parties,
still goes out with her colleagues
and old friends from college.

She works part-time,
making a difference,
in an old house by the river;
feels the pinch of recession,
and is angry with the government.

In her forties, she is not
free in a foreign country;
working in bars,
waking up on friends' couches
and in other people's beds,
or in a tent on an island
in the summer.
It is likely she too
has a beautiful brass bed,
but sleeps in it
every night –
or at least, in half of it,
and cannot be a starfish
or sleep diagonal.

Maybe she dreams
of fjords, and Northern Lights,
of Indian reservations,
of twins, and musicians,
or moving to the west of Ireland;
but she goes there every summer
to the same rented cottage,
so her children have the sea
as part of their childhood
like she did.

Of this I am certain:
She is a poet, too;
I wonder what she writes about,
and if she ever
thinks of me.

Pachelbel's Canon and Darth Vader's Theme

For two weeks, we had huddled
inside the rain, waiting
for the season to begin,
back then, when summer,
an Irish roulette of chance,
was all the work we had
to see us through a winter.

Then, that day,
on the cliff, above the rock pools,
we sat all afternoon
in the sunshine,
with sky and sea
no better shade of blue,
Beans and Erin playing 'cello,
and none of us
with anything to do
but watch the tide
move slowly out, and in,
the sound of waves and music
punctuated by
the cracking open of a beer.

Comrades in a tourist trade,
friendships forged
from an international crew;
somehow, through the hours
and hours and hours
and hours of work
as waitresses, musicians,
chefs, and barstaff,
we always made it through;
I remember saying at the time to Dave
when we hated every minute,
we'll look back and laugh, and this will be
the time we will remember
that began
for better or for worse,
with two 'cellos by the shore
in unexpected sunshine,
the Summer of Fire.

The Mermaid

for Michelle 60

Never, not again, not me,
heart bandaged with regret;
now tides come in to wet my shoes,
my steps are free
to dreaming futures in my head
that twirl in diamond drops of rain,
lithe and light, brush past my cheek,
remind me how to dance
in stockinged feet,
waltzing over morning dew,
and gliding down the puddled streets,
I'll splash through every cobbled crack,
slide down the shine of velvet rocks
beside a western sea;
no longer fear the sharpest press
of knives and tears,
sacrifices stumbled through;
there's water here to walk upon,
knowing now the earth of you.

Paddy the Giraffe

for Dad

I can see him now,
quoting Kavanagh on the lawn
to stilly greeny pensioners,
his silver pill box
forgotten on a deckchair.

Forever in his head
on holiday on Inis Mór,
when we visit, he will only
speak in Irish, the kind
with dots over the letters;
and taking us aside, whisper
of the guns that might have been
left by the Rebels in the attic
when they sold the family home.

He'll stage an early morning ambush
on the milkman,
insisting on the return
of cream-topped bottles;
give out about the *aul' ones*
who surround him,
and the women in his reading group
who never finish books;
and sneaking to the kitchen,
write *seagull* on the chicken soup –
Because they're fed on fishmeal!
he'll declare.

His pre-emptive strike is made;
one day coming home with brochures
for Park Avenue Retirement Home
in his native Sandymount,
and knowing every back lane,
is already
planning his escape.

Good Drying Out

for Mum

How many of us now
get to be our mothers
for a day?

Morning slipping out of dressing-gowns
to bring the kids to school,
return to blessed silence,
start upstairs, making beds,
ironing over radio talk,
humming songs from the kitchen sink,
clothes dancing outside
in the wind, the family pegged,
all there, in socks and shirts.

Maybe today
I'll change the sheets, or I'll dust,
sweep rugs, or mend;
as sunlight moves around the house,
time to peel potatoes, light the fire,
bake the bread;
the hours dried and folded
into drawers – by evening,
everything in its place.

Ticking Boxes

We should have got married,
in hindsight, perhaps,
although neither of us cared
for that sort of thing
at the time.
At the weddings of friends,
how we laughed at being asked
to give them all a day out;
we were the perfect couple
that other couples talked about
at dinner parties,
until we weren't,
and that was sad,
but amicably, fine.

But now it annoys me
when filling out forms,
when I have to tick
the *Single* box,
it feels like
there's something else
I'd rather be;
Divorced! and dangerous,
a loose cannon in society,
if I talked
too long to husbands,
the women would get nervous,
and the benefit of my experience,
younger men would seek out.

There should be another
cooler category
for people like me,
who have lived inside
another life,
another word beside
a little square,
that bears witness to
the joyful weight
of all those years
living in sin,
and then, again,
choosing to be free.

Telemark, July 2013

I lived so long
with open spaces,
I don't notice the sky
the way city people do.
Sitting on the porch
of this old house
looking out on trees and mountains
while young swallows
skim the morning grass
I find I think of you,
my old companion
for adventure;
and, for all those years,
it's good to sometimes miss you,
though we speak a different language now.

And swallows are always everywhere,
rehearsing flight in arcs and turns,
for autumn when they gather, fly
where they have never been,
and yet, they find their way.

Tåsen

Now, it is morning,
in the garden.

It has lost
the blasted scape
it had, just after
the snow;
green will always win.

The first signs of spring
are white and purple
flowers, in the brown.

This house has welcomed me,
last night, I lit a fire,
and watched the open flames.

From the veranda,
we view the mountains,
forest, city,
looking out over
other peoples' lives,
living too far
from the sea.

Wild Strawberries

There is a place
in the garden where
wild strawberries grow,
I come home late
in early morning,
sit for a moment
on the doorstep, thinking,
four more weeks
before I leave;
then reach across
to sample
these tiny,
juicy things.

I remember a story,
a friend of a friend,
who woke up
in a hospital in China,
speaking
three languages,
and could still
play the saxophone;
everything else
he couldn't remember,
had to learn the world
all over again.
I asked, what was the thing
that surprised him the most?
My friend said,
the taste of strawberries.

I feel a familiar
sweetness
on my tongue,
and wonder,
will something ever be
that new,
and delicious,
again,
for me?

All in a Day's Work

In a house in Potato Creek,
Gwen sits with her walking frame, patiently
waiting for a bathroom, as we
drill in screws for a bathtub surround,
then, missing plumbing fittings, take
a round trip of eighty miles
to three hardware stores, Jerry
talking all the time, pointing out
landmarks and sundance sites,
filling us in with history
and driving off road, just for the view.

On a dirt road near Eagle's Nest Butte
two Lakota men and a little girl
have run out of gas, and they hitch
a lift to a gas station, we collect them
again on our way back around,
between intermittent thunderstorms,
we feel the breadth of the Rez,
the distance between things, seen through
cracked windscreens, and the stories,
always the stories.

Overview

I would have loved him anyway,
eyes that kept me there
all night with words and wine;
then said, let's climb the sunrise
on the hill and sing
a prayer for all the ones
below us in their beds,
the ones who'd never know
looking on that mountain,
that we were ever there.

City Lover

My friend in Paris
is always trying
to find me a French lover.
Let's play a game, she says.
Just walk up to someone
and kiss them.

Even today, as I
set out for a walk,
she says,
You can still find a lover
during the day.
But how can I think of this,
when it's the city
I'm in love with?
Walking the streets
with the same look
as a woman
rising from a bed
she knows she will return to
that evening,
and everything around her
becomes sharp
and meaningful, seen
with lover's eyes.

Église Saint-Médard

I heard the bells,
allowed myself
to get a little lost
inside the city,
and came into the church
through a side entrance
that beckoned
from the street.

Again, that holy within
smell of incense,
and quiet air, I wandered
around statues
and stained glass,
taking in the silence,
like refuge.

I thought then,
of the Catholic awe
of my childhood,
kind nuns
in a convent school,
parents' faith
in moral courage,
and sin is a humanity
that can always be forgiven.
The God I knew
held a benevolent aspect
I still half-believe in,
and so, I light a candle
to every thing, everywhere
that calls itself Love.

Bookshop Garden, Ennistymon, July 2018

I find a place
for latest things,
remember how a shoelace ties,
in strange occasions where
a loose end finds its mate,
a web on a stone wall
comes free, and glides
across a secret garden,
where we sit and swing,
and talk goes on
into the night,
loops around our lives
in candleglow,
stories in old patterns
weave, and look like new.

I changed my flights to stay
a little longer,
I water flowers,
mind the bookshop,
close and open doors
around routine
of poetry, the kiss
of cold Atlantic waters
from off the ocean's rocks;
everything is afternoon,
and easy conversation,
with friends and other poets,
dogs, French crêpes,
drinks by the riverside,
musical excursions
with thumbs and kindness
to my other towns;
then back, to sleep among the books,
a reverie of words
to shape, explain
the toss and turn of tides,
timed between surprises
of each perfect day,
and still no rain.

Charo Smokes a Cigarette

Charo Egan doesn't smoke,
but when she does,
it's movie star elegant,
a Peruvian grace
of exhaled plume, that punctuates
her Spanish song;
while Patrick Egan,
the Eponymous Publican,
holds court, and a sideways
glass of wine;
no swallow nests these days,
in the new back bar.

Their clientele,
farmers, musicians, millionaires,
and graduate bartenders
who are artists and poets,
after one too many measures
of Writers Tears,
drink our Sancerre
tonight, after the pub,
from plastic cups,
down on Liscannor pier
like teenagers, singing songs,
with Midge's handmade mandolin,
forgetting all the words
of Craigie Hill,
we banter with the sea and stars,
and the bould Mick Flynn,
a summer night that lasts
three hundred years,
in the town of Tír na n-Óg,
we stay on the horse,
and never grow old.

Seeing Different Stars, Aotearoa

On the island of Rēkohu, where
the sun in the east rises first:
My last night there,
on the steps of the marae,
I finally saw
the clouds, like curtains, part to dark
on a stage, still empty
of an almost waning moon,
the stars, in strange
splendour
a spread of lights
from the bottom end
of the galaxy.

I felt like falling,
held on
by the gravity
of my situation,
not knowing
the stories of their shapes,
the legends of why
they were there;
no sisters of the Pleiades,
no Plough, not my own
September roaring bear.

Our patterns of belonging
to this planet
of land and sea,
the reasons
that we have, and how
we make our travels
are assumed accordingly,
under what is given
as a constant, from above,
that just isn't
there,
or if they are,
they're upside down,
like me
on the other side
of the sphere,
within a universe
that doesn't know
which end is up,
or doesn't care.

Things with Feathers

Falling in love
with the sound
of your voice,
like the songbird
who wakes us
in the morning, between
a corner of light
and the windowpane.

I slide out of your warmth,
bare feet on bare boards,
to put a record on,
wear your t-shirt
to make breakfast, served
with messy hair
and shiny eyes.

We, who are almost young,
though seasoned with adventures,
are shy of new beginnings,
but still can bounce on beds
and pillow fight;
yoga keeps us eloquent,
and poetry makes us supple,
enough for what could be,
as we maintain
a studied naivety.

Scattered Showers

The Little Differences

A suitcase for a holiday
in Ireland
takes in the spectrum
from Aran jumper to bikini,
which may go a way
to explaining the chaotic charm
of the mindset
of the population.

In Norway, the seasons
are much more predictable,
they trust a weather forecast
like they trust
their government.
If they say it will rain
at 12.00 on Tuesday
it will;
meanwhile, in Shannon
tourists arriving are told,
if you don't like the weather,
just wait a minute.

Still Water

We watched the pale horizon
put an end to our night,
my hand entwined in your fingers
that I long to memorize,
shared rug over shoulders,
out across the lake
a bird flies like a sign
I cannot read, this land
not being mine.
I look to you, distracted at once
by the shape of your mouth, your eyes,
everything aches,
as though already gone.
And when you speak
your voice moves like a bow
across my spine,
exquisite chords
of longing only we will know
beyond this moment,
almost time to go.

Where Were You When...

He shot John Lennon!
So the cop was told,
arriving at the scene;
I was nine years old.
I asked my babysitter,
what will happen
to the Beatles now?
She told me
they broke up years ago.

The nuns taught us 'Imagine'
in school, like a hymn
we'd never learnt before;
my teacher Miss O'Mahony
taught us the Tuiseal Ginideach,
but not on her guitar.
That summer,
she went off to teach in Africa,
we were all sad when
she decided to stay.
A bright-colour world
arrived on a postcard
she sent to me, saying
'keep smiling'.

The Angels Stop to Listen

for Sharon

Your dreaming spirit
must have woken
fifty miles away
to the noise we made
coming in,
and, sensing a reunion,
travelled south;
there was a ghost
in the guitars,
within the chords
and voice of every song,
a higher harmony,
like when the wind joins in.

I missed you then,
for times the passing angels
paused, to fill a room
with their sacred silence,
hold their breath,
just to hear you sing.

Snowglobe

I broke it
hearts and all
a world
we lived inside
safe arms
and a haven
it got shaken
a shelter
within
a prism
I smashed it
using only words

I can't do this
any more

and it shattered
into a different
kind of freedom

Substance

Measure the bottle
after I leave,
see what I took;
the matter
of my body
will never be
a constant,
so much depends
on an evening,
the music played,
and how heavy
the heart can weigh.

Moonfish Café

Working in the café
feels like always
waiting for someone
to turn up —
because usually,
someone does.

Mostly other colleagues
for coffee, or a staff-price beer;
open summer days,
sitting on a smoke break,
outside, by the river,
looking up to catch
a familiar figure
against the sunlight
crossing Beier Bridge;
we wave, draw down
another one
to come and join us
in our evening routines,
and other dramas.

But there are long days
with only customers,
and quiet Sunday nights
when no one comes at all;
and locking up alone
a large, empty building,
I walk through halls
with ghosts of weddings
and nocturnal celebrations;
and further back in time,
the walls remember
the spirits of the factory girls,
the rush of waterfall
in their ears, and in mine
now, the only witness
in the darkness;
how I came to be here,
so suddenly aware of
the loneliness of chance.

After Hours

These old buildings,
sensitive, like us,
to daylight,
contain our anger
at the world,
and turn it into
something else;
surrounded now
by quiet snow,
they remember rains
of blossoms,
falling leaves,
and summer laughter
caught
in fragile seasons.

They are haunted by
our present dramas,
we are
their future ghosts.

How we have played
out the music
of the Night People,
belonging, in these hours,
only to ourselves;
laws that begin
in the morning
meet us, going home,
form no part
of words spoken
between the walls
where everything
can be forgiven,
just because
judgement is asleep.

How intoxicating,
and how dangerous.

The Terrorists Have Won

This town has gone septic,
Rules have crept in,
no place
for leeway
or loophole.
The Paranoid
are burning their diaries,
lawyering up
for Worst Case Scenario,
afraid of the evidence
on grainy footage
that Government officials
shall monitor;
telling us now
It's For Our Own Good
and Won't Somebody
Think of the Children.

The Fun Police
are on patrol,
their maps marked in red
of every last stronghold
in hidden corners
where the party
might still
be going on;
their special agents
send in the SWAT teams,
tell grown ups,
it's time you were in bed.

Chastized, curtailed, counted,
in the Name of Progress
and computerization
we are permutized, homogenized,
systemized,
though nothing
bad has happened yet,

but oh, the threat that it might;
a people controlled
by feeding their fear
as we walk home at night
before Curfew
on the Streets of Terror,
no one sees
that side of sunrise
any more.

...And Both Bars On

You won't be unhappy
with the decision that you made.
You are years from now,
remembering, slightly differently,
each time you pull it back,
the clothes you wore that day,
which one of you said what.

That pivot of a time –
a certain smell, a song you hear,
the way the light
can catch an hour,
shocks a sudden piece of you
that still lives there,
the reminding
of a different choice,
one still also lonely
in old walls, and other souls;
but in the end, you either
left
or stayed –
created new adventures
you could never
be without,
or dug down
where you stood, found
what you were looking for –
and each way
gave you pain.

Now, you will never
know the difference
that it makes,
or get the chance
to choose again.

Little Victories

This soft spring rain
that falls tonight,
must be taken slowly,
gentle, not to drench us, but
misty, under lamplight;
we walk out into it
from an old easy building,
having stretched our time,
lengthened
into more conversation.
You asked me
was I going home,
as if it might not be a given,
but tomorrow, as you knew,
I had things to do,
but walked away
still smiling.

And like the rain,
there is a sense of trust
that wakens
in weather like this,
a kind of honesty
I had almost forgotten;
as if this is enough
to start to see things differently,
just knowing, maybe now,
or soon,
winter will be over.

The Smell of Earth After Rain

There comes a time
when it comes down
to the little things
you notice
when the big things go away;
it's suddenly summer,
with its green lush of life,
a purity
that stops you speaking,
just so you can listen,
both feet on the ground,
present, within a body,
like your heartbeat
is the only thing that matters.

It's on its way,
hasn't quite arrived,
but, oh, that moment,
just before it happens,
and somehow,
you already knew.

Summer Sounds

There is one beat strange
my heart gives
when something unexpected
connects me to you.

How different should
this city feel
when I know
you're not in it?
Does it become
something else,
do I feel free?

I still look for you
where I'd expect
to find you,
everything seems out of tune,
and there is no other music
that understands me.

Something in August

It comes in the air,
a sound in the leaves,
the sun's whisper
of a paler idea,
an unresolved question
we were taking
all summer to answer;
cold breath
on tips of fingers,
creeping over browned skin
under stars, as we sleep.

The sea takes on
a sharper, darker hue,
this change, too soon,
for all the shorter shadows,
longer hours,
and brighter plans
to follow through.

Out of Key

There's a house
I don't enter any more,
the keys are gone from me,
and even if they were
still on some ring
sounding like a bell
in my handbag,
they would open a door
to a different place,
some stranger's face,
and I would be a guest
delayed, following an old address
for the former occupant,
be told,
I'm sorry, but she's gone.
Yet in the garden,
the flowers still grow.

The Smaller Picture

for Estlin Luna

A photograph that catches
unaware, something
beautiful, but at the time,
seemed inconsequential,
or mundane;
just before the moment
when everything changed.

A precious carelessness
that dwelt inside a day,
barely noticed, nothing
worthy of a frame;
the furiousness of loss
to see that ease,
so casually captured
in shutter-speed.

How devastating now
to think it could
have continued, as it had,
what else would we have done,
held how much closer,
if we'd known
our hearts are only ever
out on loan.

Nothing to do with Weather

The task
of guarding hearts
against the tragedy of us
is somehow mirrored
like a poem
in translation
on an opposite page,
a book's spine
in between;
the backbone
and the courage
that it took
to be separate,
but will forever
close into conversation
and save us from each other,
and all the while go on
meaning the same thing.

Flight Path

Planes fly
in invisible arcs
like bridges
between places,
form a brief
and tender road,
where parting sadness
moves, in midair,
morphs into
some kind of arriving.

Me, still on the ground,
spinning, and unravelling
a tight ball
of coloured threads,
pulling them apart
to tie up
the loose ends.

My books, and my
collections
of things, and those,
whose eyes hold a look
I've come to depend on;
an open empty suitcase,
I wonder what will fit,
and wonder how
I can leave
at all.

But I will pull
the front door shut
with all the house asleep,
breathe in
the fragile air
of dawn,
put my bag
on my back,
and move on.

Legacy

Do not bury me
in the earth,
the land is for
the living.

Burn me
so I don't decay,
so I go the way
of ancestors,
and witches,
sharp and ending,
complete.

Give each grandchild
ashes
and an adventure –
go there
to the places
I have loved –

take me to the island;

take a boat out
into an ocean's bay;

climb a mountain
just to see
the distance of the prairies;

find that bar,
and pour me
into an ashtray
that only comes out
after closing time.

Funeral Rain

Crossing the bridge over the dual carriageway, I noticed a tiny plaque: 'Blithe Spirit', it said, with a set of dates that I totted up as lacking a decade of Cara's. The story suddenly came back to me: a laughing girl who'd tightroped along the handrail one night and tripped to her death in the traffic below. I traced the lettering with a fingertip. Was she drunk, or usually lucky, was that what made her try it? And what were we to do with these Achillean types, these careless losers of life, when there seemed no way of locking them up, strapping them down, forcing them to take only the risks the rest of us considered worth it?

from *Hood* by EMMA DONOGHUE

Nesodden, November 2018

Shaken from strange dreams,
strange, because
in dreams I wasn't loved,
I take
a coffee out
to the back porch, where
the rocks slope down
to the impossible beauty
of a blue ice-morning sky,
reflected, bright and heavy
on a molten, rippled sea,
and quietly,
light eases through
silver-frosted branches,
empties out unknowns
of past and futures,
breathing in the gold
of winter sun
that says,
a presence on this earth
is not forgotten, nothing
is ever forgotten.

Today, that sun
has somehow risen
just to shine alone,
with me as only witness,
to remind me.

Flowers on the Bridge

My life once
poured through your death
like the focus
of a funnel;
I placed new value
on October air,
the crunch of leaves,
the time used up
not noticing
that clouds are different
every day,
and each minute
is a different colour.

Eighteen years stopped short
on a bridge you never crossed,
but joking, leaning, falling,
over some other boundary
onto the road beneath;
blood like a halo
around your head.
You made the morning papers,
full of talk of ballerinas,
a paragraph
was all you got,
and the rest of the world
turned the page.

But your spirit
I carry with me
like a smiling photo
taken to the trenches;
and I still dream
I catch you,
but you always laugh
and turn away,
and never say goodbye;

those small rebellions
like memory,
years shrunk to fit
your image in
a frame around you,
in how many rooms,
laughing from our
walls and shelves,
like a bird before flight.

Siamese Twins

After, people told me,
when they heard the news,
they thought of me:
Oh no, what will Jean do now?
A kindred spirit
in formative years
can never be replaced,
even with a thousand friends;
the answer to that question is,
it fades, and then it spins.

April, 1979

When I see ghosts, I see
a little girl tumbling
on the bars of a swing-set,
over and over, like the loop
of that first memory
of her
in the garden next door,
at Eithne's birthday party
when we were eight;
a gymnast in a red
velvet dress, pale,
with long black hair.
I can't remember
if we spoke, that day,
I only recall
the energy of lithe movement,
long, skinny legs
twirling and spinning
over into air.

Tormenting the Nuns

We went to the same secondary school,
where her mother was a boarder in her youth;
Sion Hill, Blackrock, down the road from me
and across the road from her.
When she was late, Miss O'Dwyer would quip,
Miss the bus again, Julie?
2 Silver, in the Matchbox,
where, when it rained,
it leaked through the windows,
and we moved our desks
away from the walls.
There, we learned to smoke
behind the hockey pitch
down by the nuns' graveyard,
trying to be cool –
but we never really were
like the girls who had boyfriends
and who were allowed to go to discos.

At sixteen, our names turned into one,
JeanandJulie, always together,
breaking all the rules;
we stole the key
for the roof of St Thomas's,
where with glee, we ate our lunch
looking down from four floors up,
at everyone else on the hockey pitch,
and made faces through the skylights
at our classmates below;
stuck chewing gum in locks of doors
of rooms we wanted access to,
we snuck into the nuns' quarters,
the secret gallery of the school chapel,
the Harp Room, the Red Stairs,
the fire escapes, everywhere
that was out-of-bounds;

turned the giant crucifix in the library
upside-down,
the nuns were freaked out
at the thought of a Satanic sect,
but it was just JeanandJulie,
having the craic;
the small rebellions
within a convent school.

Diary, 1990

I.

The twelfth of October feels now like a liquid dream half-remembered scenes of someone else's film but also like a film you watched over and over like we used to watch The Breakfast Club or The Slipper and the Rose a night like any other like any one of hundreds of nights going out a Friday night the first one back at college we were all heading up to the UCD bar on the phone that afternoon to Julie we arranged that I should call down to her at eight o'clock and we would get the number 17 bus up to UCD Bryan had rung her to say he'd be working late and couldn't come he'd had some sort of fuck-up on the computer I walked down Merrion Avenue to her house on Waltham Terrace Jules was in the downstairs bathroom finishing off her make-up when I arrived and made some comment about wearing the same clothes she'd been wearing all day black jeans and purple shirt I laughed and reminded her I hadn't been in college that day so I didn't notice we went upstairs to her bedroom where clothes lay scattered all over the place obviously she'd been deciding 'what to wear' before we left she took a small half-empty bottle of vodka out from under the bed asked my advice on what coat she should wear and we left we crossed the road to McCabe's on the way we met her Dad and he wished us well on our night out I remember thinking what if that was the last time he ever saw us like a premonition we went next door to Straney's to get cigarettes and to see if Michele was working then crossed the road to the bus stop as we had a few minutes to spare we walked up the avenue to the next stop and stayed there for a while chatting though I can't remember what about I remember her talking about Bryan being sick and how there was no point in him lying to her because she could always tell I counted my change wondering if I would get away with 45p Julie said that it was 45p from the next stop the one outside my road so for the sake of 20p we decided to jog up to it we needn't have bothered running as we had to wait a few more minutes but it came at last and we got on Ailbe Suzanne and Laoise were at the stop at the top of the avenue they sat in the seats behind us and Laoise handed out straws we got out at UCD and headed straight for the bar the plan was this we'd stay a while and see the band and then head out to Stradbrook where Johnny Lavin had organized a college disco

The Sound of Music

The school put on a musical
every second year,
and for *The Sound of Music*,
JeanandJulie
ruled backstage.
We got ourselves out of class
for every rehearsal,
and to help Miss O'Rafferty
paint the backdrops
because we did Art;
us, in our black Levi's 501 jeans,
moving props around,
knowing every word
to every song.

Miss Stephens taught us
the four-part harmonies
of 'the hills are alive'
in choir, and we sang them
later, to the sea;
we had our other favourites
too, and watched the film
every second day,
imitating Christopher Plummer's
bad jokes, and twirling like Liesl
in the gazebo;
both of us
and the whole school
were obsessed
those weeks;
no other music
was heard.

Diary, 1990

Eithne and Justin were there already along with Shane and Dave I saw John and Peter down the other end near the band I went up to the bar with Laoise and ordered a Southern Comfort and red and she got a bottle of lime the barman eyed her suspiciously and asked had she got her own drink and she lied and said she lived on campus then myself Julie Laoise and Suzanne went out to a picnic table outside so Sha and Jules could drink their illegal vodka and Bacardi they were in mad moods Suzanne and myself were acting more sober probably because we knew we were staying that way due to lack of funds when their bottles were empty Julie and Laoise threw their bottles over the fence at the same time to see if they would smash together but the bottles went in completely opposite directions and we laughed then we went back inside I'm not sure if Justin or Shane and Dave had left at this point but they left soon after we were down the other end of the bar with Ailbe John and Peter and sat around near the band that was playing then myself and Laoise got chatting to three guys from her economics class and they gave us a couple of cans of Heineken Laoise disappeared somewhere with one and I talked to the other two bringing them over to the rest of my friends the others seemed to be heading off Suzanne and Eithne went to find Laoise while Natasha Cora Debs and Julie were making their way outside I remember calling after Julie feeling a sudden urgency to go with her but she didn't hear me and didn't turn around my last memory of her was seeing her moving away towards the front door of the bar for some reason I decided to hang on for Eithne and Suzanne to come back with Laoise

And Veritas Shall Be Our Rule

The worst thing we ever did,
was bunk off school on a sunny day,
way too sunny
to be in school, stupid because
we had the same classes
that afternoon, and they'd notice
neither of us were there;
but the sea called us,
we ran, and danced in the waves
in our school uniforms
on Blackrock beach, by our little pier
and the nineteenth-century folly ruins.
They couldn't prove
we left the school grounds,
they interviewed us separately,
but we had our story straight.

Then, they called our parents in,
and my mother said,
I raised my child with integrity,
I believe her, she wouldn't lie.
So I learned my lesson early,
the Dominican way,
Veritas their motto;
the nuns said it's not
just about telling the truth,
but being true to yourself.
We lied to those we loved,
that's why
it's the worst thing we ever did.

Diary, 1990

III.

we couldn't have been more than five minutes after them and we probably walked a lot faster than they did the others had eventually found Laoise we were walking in pairs Eithne and Suzanne in front myself and Laoise behind we crossed the road at the college entrance over to the flyover bridge and I noticed Julie's coat lying on the ground Eithne and Suzanne went on ahead I picked it up assuming Julie had dropped it she was always losing jackets I said in a loud voice to Laoise oh look it's Julie's coat she must have dropped it I was thinking happily she would be thrilled to get it back at Stradbrook there were a group of people nearby I didn't know who they were I just remember a girl's voice saying something like your friend's on the dual carriageway I think she's dead

At Seventeen

How the world opened up
for us then, when we learned
that boys could be
our friends;
after that,
the group dynamic changed,
to JeanandJulie
and All the Guys.

We learned to drink together,
or rather, Julie taught me;
I was all Curehead depression,
she was all, *Let's go out and have fun!*
So out we went, in black clothes
and purple lipstick,
dancing to the Doors, the Cure, INXS,
and our favourite DJ, Ronan, who always
played 'Peace Frog' for us.
The boys played in bands,
and covered the Beatles, the Who and the Jam,
and a rocking version of
'A Hazy Shade of Winter',
one of *our* songs,
me with all my
unpublished rhyme,
and Julie's drink became
vodka and lime;
underage drinking in the Underground
on Saturday afternoons.

Walking home at night
from Blackrock, or Clonskeagh,
and standing on a beach to wait
for a sunrise that never came,
too many Irish clouds in the way,
it just got a brighter grey.
So we ended up waltzing
up dotted lines, in the middle
of Mount Merrion Avenue,
too early for cars,
but felt the danger anyway.

Diary, 1990

IV.

I didn't have to try too hard to guess what had happened I knew Julie and it wasn't the first time she'd messed about leaning over bridges I ran to the railings and looked down onto the road below I couldn't see a body of any sort but there were people standing around and I recognized the top of Natasha's head I started running across the bridge after Eithne and Suzanne who were running for the approaching bus I shouted at them something about Julie being on the dual carriageway and the four of us ran down the slope across the road and towards the crowd of people I was out of breath and thought oh shit I probably am pregnant and I was but didn't know that yet and the others got ahead of me and as I drew nearer I could see a black and purple form stretched out on the road I got within about twenty feet of her before I saw the pool of blood around her head and as I watched it stopped spreading I knew then that Julie was either dead or would never recover completely I couldn't go much nearer I could hardly gulp in any air I started screaming out her name in terror and hands grabbed me whispering in my ear that my friend was going to be alright I couldn't handle the empty reassurance and turned away in panic Peter was there and the familiar face calmed me down I had to stop being hysterical I couldn't help Julie that way I kept saying to myself be calm be calm you can freak out later I went as near to Julie as I could bring myself to I was too afraid of the blood of what it meant I was afraid I'd see her brains spill out on the ground or something I kept wishing it hadn't been her head why her head

Sundays

Sundays were our day
for walking down on Blackrock beach,
and sitting on the pier, or climbing rocks,
strolling around the park,
or hanging out in Blackrock Market,
chatting to the stallholders,
buying jewellery, or art;
or cycling up to Tim's when we
were supposed to be at evening Mass,
as he converted us to Guns N' Roses,
singing 'I Used to Love Her',
as we freewheeled
down the hill home.

That last Sunday,
I called to her house
in the afternoon,
and burst into tears on her doorstep,
and she gave me a hug;
I asked her,
If I am pregnant, will you be godmother?
Thinking, at the time,
it was the worst thing
that could happen
to either of us.

Diary, 1990

V.

Cora was kneeling beside her holding her hand and I remember talking to Cora asking if she could feel a pulse the ambulance arrived and I asked if I could go with her in it at first the ambulance men said no we'd be in the way and I watched them turn Julie over and put her on a stretcher then the ambulance man let myself and Cora get in and Julie followed I remember the relief in seeing that her face was still okay there was just a lot of blood on it but I couldn't see a source her hand still had all her rings on it the one that I could see the man put a tube down her throat and gave her oxygen I heard the ambulance siren from the inside I was in that ambulance he asked did she have false teeth I said no but one of her front teeth had a crown it had got broken in a toboggan accident in the snow one year I guess that was too much information I was babbling he then asked her name address was she a student and then suddenly we were turning into Saint Vincent's accident and emergency building I couldn't believe it was so quick the ambulance man told us to be ready to jump out and clear the way and as soon as the ambulance stopped we did the others arrived in the taxi that had stopped when she fell and blocked the road in front of her to warn other cars and we stood and watched Julie being wheeled past us and inside

Bryan's Car

I'm not saying Bryan was shallow,
that the reason he gave us lifts
was because my two best friends,
Julie and Eithne,
just happened to be
the best-looking girls in Dublin;
yes, he may have enjoyed
walking into our nightclub
with the hot chicks on his arm,
but Bryan was sensitive,
and grieving two brothers,
so we looked after him, too.

There were rules to Bryan's car:
    a) Don't take Bryan's car for granted;
    b) Bryan's car, Bryan's music;
    c) Never question the bizarre or wayward route
       of the order of progression
       that Bryan drove us home,
       Julie was always last.

Then she asked him
to make it permanent,
and they fell in love;
and she rode shotgun
all that summer.

On other nights, Bryan would drive us
up the Dublin mountains
to see the city lights below
out to the sea, and stars above,
with Bryan's soundtracks
our theme tunes,
everything from *Vogue*
to *Violator*, all the way
to Connemara, and Renvyle,
our last holiday.

But the songs I remember most
were the ones he played
between church and cemetery,
following a big black car,
and oh, the rain that day;
the heavens lashed
down their sympathy
on us, driving to bury
something in the ground
too special,
that shouldn't go there,
and that journey
lasted years;
with A-ha, we faced the rain,
and the Cure's 'A Night Like This'
reminded us of
that Friday night before,
while the rhythm of the strings
in 'Cloudbusting'
kept time with windscreen wipers;
and it's Kate Bush I think of
every time it rains,
and here in my head
I'm back there again,
a passenger of grief
in Bryan's car.

Diary, 1990

VI.

there were five of us myself Eithne Cora Natasha and Debs then Suzanne and Laoise arrived a short while after we followed the stretcher in and I went to reception and gave all Julie's details I didn't know the name of her GP I asked if I could ring Julie's parents rather than have a stranger do it the guy said no first we argued then he went to check it out and came back and said it was okay someone gave me change and I rang from a payphone on the wall Mr Ryan answered 'Mr Ryan this is Jean we're in Vincent's I'm afraid Julie's had an accident' there was a pause 'What happened?' 'She fell off a bridge' 'What??' 'The bridge outside UCD — she fell. Can you come down? We're in the emergency area' 'Okay — thank you Jean, we'll be down' I hung up, thanking the receptionist and went outside to the others Debs and Natasha were hysterical Debs was crying and blaming herself for not being able to stop her going over and Eithne was trying to calm her down the ambulance man came out with a bucket of water and started cleaning the blood from the walls and the floor of the ambulance I went up to him to see if he knew anything I watched him scrubbing down the wall and the door 'Is there any chance of brain damage?' I asked he looked up 'Every chance of it, yeah' I asked how long it would be before they knew he said an hour or two 'Well at least she's still alive' I said smiling he looked straight at me with an expression and didn't answer then he went back inside with the basin of bloody water Julie's blood

Friday Shoppers

for Ailbe

I have the photos still
of that famous afternoon,
the three of us, in poses
down on Blackrock beach.
When earlier,
in Stillorgan Shopping Centre,
we were discovered,
our fingers gouging ginger cake,
mouths full,
sitting on a bench,
by my mother, laughing,
out to do her weekly shop;
Like tramps, she said, of us.

Long after, coming from the funeral,
watching shoppers go about
in all their cruel normality;
jealous that they dared to laugh,
that friends were all accounted for;
how could such a monumental crack
not shake the mirrors with her fall,
a quake that should have left
no heart intact.

The two of us now left,
of those who dressed in teenage black
amid our brightly coloured friends,
are bonded by a wander
down a supermarket aisle;
reaching for Jamaica Ginger Cake,
three childlike, greedy smiles.

Diary, 1990

VII.

It seemed like an age waiting for the Ryans to arrive I went out to the car park in case they didn't know where to come but eventually the Ovlov drew up I went over and said hello I thought they would have a million questions but Mr Ryan just nodded and Mrs Ryan walked straight ahead as if in a dream I guess the questions would come later they went inside and we could see them through the doors standing waiting it was a while before someone came out and brought them in to where we thought Julie was myself and Suzanne went to get change for the coffee machine and as we were walking down the hospital corridors the clocks told me it was midnight I told Suzanne what the ambulance man said and didn't say and that it seemed unlikely Julie would make a complete recovery she seemed calm enough to talk to like that we met up with the others and went back to the waiting room Laoise was in bits she just kept crying I was completely calm we weren't there long before a nurse came in and told us to go home that we couldn't do anything else that Julie was 'critical' she ushered us firmly outside I had to go back in for someone's jacket and Julie's shoe was on a chair beside it someone had brought it from the scene of the accident I stood there holding it helplessly wondering what to do with a shoe of Julie's the ambulance man said gently 'I'll take it'

I went outside to join the others Peter and a couple of others arrived as we crossed the car park we told them we'd been asked to leave and all we knew was that Julie was 'critical'

We were back in Suzanne's apartment on Merrion Avenue before I realized I was still holding Julie's coat

Paris and Jim

A line in a film I once saw, said
Everyone, eventually, ends up
either dead or pregnant.

We had two good excuses
not to be in Paris
in the Summer of '91,
living and working, between college terms,
and for Jim's 20th anniversary
in Père Lachaise.

How we had planned it,
along with
our future selves,
under high ceilings
in a shared apartment
on Idron'e Terrace, where
we'd look out on Howth,
and take on the world.

We had different
ambitions of lights:
yours, the Aurora Borealis;
mine, a winter solstice sunrise
lighting the inner chamber
at Newgrange.

But our dreams of Europe
were the same;
travelling on trains,
net curtains and brass beds
in attic rooms in cities,
whitewashed villas by
a Mediterranean sea,
meeting other souls
on dusty mountain roads,
singing around firesides
in snowy valleys, how

we'd take exotic lovers,
who would give us stories
to bring home again,
we'd live it
as it came,
and consider, after,
all it meant.
What escapades and adventures
two best friends would have had
in our twenties,
instead,
we'll never
even have Paris.

Diary, 1990

VIII.

Suzanne's mother was a nurse who worked nights so we had somewhere to go and be together in the apartment and someone went down to get the others from Stradbrook who had got on the bus from UCD before anything happened then at some point Suzanne's mother came back and myself and Eithne took a walk down Merrion Avenue to get some air and sat on a bench by South Hill Avenue to try to make sense of everything and as we walked back up to the apartment my mother and Eithne's mother were standing there on the front doorstep and everyone was crying and I said she's dead isn't she and the worst thing was we had to go back upstairs to everyone up there and tell them all Julie's friends and I remember the long walk down the corridor and Suzanne walking towards me from the apartment door and I think I said something like she's gone and I remember the boys coming in from Stradbrook and Ailbe just looking at me and saying there's only two of us left now and I knew what he meant but I don't remember everything now just that apartment holding in its walls the explosion of the news that destroyed all of us and our little world along with it

Witness Statement

Statement of Peter McDonald, 3 Sycamore Crescent, Mount Merrion, Co. Dublin made to Garda Matthew Nyland of Donnybrook Garda Station, at 24 Grove Lawn, Blackrock on the 14.10.'90

I am a student at U.C.D. Belfield, studying for an Arts Degree. I am in first year. On the night of the 12.10.'90 a group of us including Julie Ryan were in the bar at Belfield. We had been there since around 9 p.m. Julie had been drinking but I don't know what. At about 11.15 p.m. we decided to leave the bar as we were going to catch the bus because we were going to the disco in Stradbrook, Blackrock. I was in the same group as Julie leaving the bar. Everyone was in good form, especially Julie. When we got to the fly-over bridge I was about 7-8 ft. behind Julie. We had to cross the bridge to get to the bus stop which was on the Montrose Hotel side of the dual carriageway. I saw Julie at the railings on the south side of the bridge. She put her feet between the vertical railings on the bridge. She then put both arms over the top horizontal railing and grabbed hold of the two vertical railings on the other side, so she was leaning over the bridge at this stage. She pushed a little more forward and her feet came away from between the railings. Her body tipped forward too much and she lost balance. Her legs went up in the air and fell forward over the bridge and she disappeared. I remember suddenly thinking that a car might run over her on the roadway underneath so I ran down the slipway through the shrubbery onto the dual carriageway. She had fallen under the bridge onto the roadway on the southern side of the inward road. She was in the middle lane. She was lying face down on the roadway. I stood in front of her to stop cars running over her. A taxi stopped and I asked him to call an Ambulance and he said he had already done so. An Ambulance arrived shortly. Julie showed no sign of life whatsoever. There was a pool of blood on the roadway at her head. The whole thing happened in the space of a couple of seconds. I have had this statement read over to me and it is correct. I do not wish to make any alterations or additions to it.

Signed: Peter McDonald
Witness: Garda Matthew Nyland
Dated: 14.10.'90

Nothing Bad Ever Happens in Tiffany's

One day, someone
will take me to New York;
they will bring me to Tiffany's
and buy me
a platinum diamond
solitaire.

Not because
I love shiny things,
and I once worked
in a jeweller's,
and I adore Audrey Hepburn;
they might want
to marry me,
and if so, should
ask me there;
mostly it's because
of the girl who taught me
how to play
'Moon River' on the piano,
and we joked, as
teenage girls will do:
if one of us dies,
all the other has to do
is play that song
to have the other
looking over her shoulder.

And then she did.

So every time now
I come across that instrument,
I find I've forgotten
the TV series theme tune
to *The Incredible Hulk*,
the piano solo
from 'The Crystal Ship',

and Beethoven's
Moonlight Sonata;
but long forgotten fingers
know to play
the first eight bars
of Mancini —
and so I need
a Moon River ring
as a reminder
that somehow diamonds
and a girl's best friend
have a connection,
wider than a mile.

For Sale: No. 2, Waltham Terrace

You are a house of many stairs,
how many have I sat upon,
count the years —
I may have missed one or two,
though she and I
slid down them all.
Soon,
your corner will announce a
SALE AGREED
that says to me,
YOU CAN NO LONGER ENTER
just like her buried heart,
lost to me.

A Thursday newspaper —
your photograph, you are a
*Rarely Does A House Like This
Come on The Market.*
I imagine then, from the return,
'Moon River' on a piano
that isn't there.

Your Regency aesthetic
I'd built my past upon;
calling to your door
she opened up to me
that last time, that night,
running out to catch the bus,
all smiles.

Only hours after,
I was arguing with nurses,
to let me make that phone
ring in your hall,
to save her family
the measured words
of tactful strangers.

And all the years after,
calling down for dinner,
chatting to her mother
as if she were only in
some other room;
times that I went looking,
peeping in the shadowed drawing-room,
the scene of childhood sleepovers,
memories your walls and I still hold –
no matter how we're reinvented,
renovated, both of us are haunted,
always seeing, from your window
framing, in the dark,
the tree, whose leaves
she always said
the streetlights turned to gold.

Hey Jules

Hey Jules, you stopped the rain
as we parked the cars
at Shanganagh Cemetery,
a rain
that had gone on for days;
I thought of bloodstains
where you fell, washed away
under the bridge, where
Detective Nyland brought me to,
getting stories straight;
I could see him
trying not to cry.

We walked you to your grave,
the air dense with birdsong
as we lowered you down,
a quilt of flowers
laid so thick
I would have almost
slept there with you.
Instead, I started singing
a song that always
meant your name,
and all your friends joined in
to make it better, quietly,
as we stood
and watched your body
disappear, knowing
we'd never forget
that song, that moment,
that October, that year.

Her Favourite Purple Shirt

Grief is a tight ball
of threads of a life
that never come undone;
the experts used to think
over time, it got smaller,
now they say
it stays the same size,
we just make
the rest of our lives
bigger around it.

How many of your
purple-coloured threads
are still curled
into every tapestry
I weave,
no matter how
I change my world,
there is always
a hue,
and if I picked one out
and followed it back,
it would lead me
through the labyrinth,
to the centre of
the absence of you.

Photograph: Aurora Hannisdal

JEAN KAVANAGH is an Irish poet living in Norway. She studied Irish Folklore and English Literature in UCD, Dublin, and has a Masters' Degree in Indigenous Studies from the Arctic University of Tromsø, Norway. Her work has been published in journals, showcase anthologies for the Galway Arts Centre, and in *Dogs Singing: A Tribute Anthology* (Salmon, 2011), and *Even the Daybreak: 35 Years of Salmon Poetry* (Salmon, 2016). In 2012 she was shortlisted for the Patrick Kavanagh Poetry Award. *Other Places*, her debut collection, was published in 2014, and was shortlisted for the Strong/Shine Award for Best First Collection in 2015.

salmonpoetry
Cliffs of Moher, County Clare, Ireland

"Like the sea-run Steelhead salmon that thrashes upstream to its spawning ground, then instead of dying, returns to the sea – Salmon Poetry Press brings precious cargo to both Ireland and America in the poetry it publishes, then carries that select work to its readership against incalculable odds."

TESS GALLAGHER

The Salmon Bookshop
& Literary Centre

Ennistymon, County Clare, Ireland

"Another wonderful Clare outlet."
The Irish Times, 35 Best Independent Bookshops